The Story of The Liberty Bell

By Natalie Miller

Illustrations by Betsy Warren

CHILDRENS PRESS, CHICAGO

Over two hundred years ago, when our country was still a part of England, the people of Pennsylvania built a fine big State House in Philadelphia.

4

"We need a good-sized bell for our steeple," said one man.

"Let us order the biggest bell in all the thirteen colonies," said another.

"And let's vote that it be made of only the finest materials." said a third.

But in that year of 1751 there was no one in America who knew how to make a bell.

So the chairman of the assembly wrote a letter to London with his best quill pen.

He asked the best bell-makers in England to make a fine bell weighing about 2000 pounds. He asked them to put one of his favorite Bible quotations on it: *Proclaim Liberty throughout all the land to all the inhabitants thereof. Lev., XXV, 10*.

The town people knew it took a long time to make a bell properly. But by summer they began watching the big ships coming in with the sun shining on the white sails.

"Maybe the bell is on that one," they said.

One day in August they were happy to hear the town crier going up and down the cobblestone streets crying, "Hear ye! Hear ye! The big bell is on the *Matilda* just arriving."

Cobblers left their benches.
Blacksmiths left their anvils.
Bakers left their ovens.
Everyone who could went down to the wharf to
see the sailors hoist the heavy bell onto a wagon.

They all agreed it was a handsome bell and they were proud of it. The crowd followed the creaking wagon with its precious cargo up the hill to the State House lawn.

Workmen built a frame on the lawn. They hung the great bell on it so that the people could see and hear it before it was raised to the steeple.

The assemblymen brought their wives in silk and satin gowns. The Quakers were there in quiet gray cotton. The wives of the tradesmen came in homespun with big white aprons.

The bellringer raised the clapper. The new bell rang out in full deep-throated tones. Everyone smiled and cheered. Once, twice it rang, and then --thud! It sounded like a dented kettle. Their beautiful big bell had cracked! What should they do!

Two men who owned an iron foundry said they would try to recast it, although they had never done such a thing before.

Iron casting and bell casting are two different things, for bells have no iron in them. They are made of tin and copper. The amount of each metal makes the tone of the bell.

The two men made a mold and then broke the bell into pieces to remelt it.

The ironmakers and some of the assemblymen decided to add a little more copper. They thought it would strengthen the bell so that it would not crack again. They did not think they were adding enough to change the tone.

When the great bell was finished it was hung in the steeple and the assemblymen ordered a big feast on the State House lawn to celebrate.

But when they rang the bell, its voice was high and unpleasant! The ironmakers would have to recast it!

The next time it was completed it was hung quietly in the tower with no celebration. For 82 years that voice spoke loudly and clearly to the good people of Philadelphia and the neighboring towns.

During the early years of its life the great bell rang often.

King George of England was trying to make the people in the colonies pay his bills by taxing them heavily. Naturally they did not like this.

So all thirteen colonies sent wise men to Philadelphia to talk over their problems. This meeting was called the Continental Congress.

It was one of the duties of the bell to call the men to their meetings. They called it the State House bell so others began calling it by that name, too.

Whenever the king added a new tax, the bell summoned the people to the State House yard to hear about it.

In 1776 the Continental Congress passed the *Declaration of Independence*. It said the colonies didn't want to belong to England any more and were willing to fight for their freedom.

When the Declaration was read to the people the bell rang so loudly and so joyously some were afraid the beams of the steeple might fall.

It continued to ring far into the night while bonfires blazed and parades filled the streets.

King George was not willing to give up his colonies without a fight, so he sent troops in bright red coats with brass buttons.

A year later word came that the hated Redcoats were about to march into Philadelphia and use it as a winter headquarters.

The patriots were afraid the enemy would melt their beloved bell into bullets. Carefully they took it from the steeple and hid it on a farmer's wagon under a load of hay.

By night, on slippery rain-soaked roads cut with deep ruts, they smuggled the bell through enemy lines.

Near Bethlehem the hard-working wagon broke down and the bell had to be lifted to another.

After a hard journey it reached Allentown. There it was hidden under the floor of the Zion Reformed Church and there it stayed for nearly a year.

When the British marched out of Philadelphia the Americans set to work cleaning up the State House. It had been used for a hospital and was left in very bad shape.

They scrubbed it with soap and sand and bushels of lime so that it would be fit for the Congress to use. Then they brought back their bell.

Even those who had complained it was too loud were happy to hear its cheerful voice again.

In 1781 it joyfully announced the end of the war with England. The United States was at last free!

In 1787 when the Constitution became the law of the land, two teams of two men each rang the bell for a huge celebration.

The bell did not have so much to do after that. It rang for holidays and to welcome honored visitors. It tolled sadly for the death of great Americans.

It was tolling for the death of Chief Justice John Marshall on July 8, 1835, when suddenly its familiar voice went dull and harsh.

The bell once more had cracked!

For over ten years it hung in the steeple silent and forgotten.

A newspaper reporter remembered it when the city was planning a wonderful celebration in honor of George Washington's birthday in 1846. He suggested the State House bell might be mended to ring for the occasion.

The men in charge liked the idea, and a work-man climbed to the tower to see what could be done. He thought that the tone might be restored if the edges of the crack did not touch each other.

For a few hours on the special holiday the great bell rang loudly and clearly, as though happy to be once more taking part in the activities of a patriotic America.

The effort was too great for it. At noon it cracked in such a way that it could never speak aloud again.

When the bell was a hundred years old it was brought down from its quiet steeple and placed on a pedestal with thirteen sides.

It was now called *Old Independence Bell* because the State House was being restored and was called *Hall of Independence.*

In 1876 Philadelphia had a big fair in honor of our country's hundred years of Independence. People came from all over the world to visit.

They flocked to see the bell because they knew the part it had played in America's fight for freedom. They began calling it affectionately *The Liberty Bell* and it has been known by that name ever since.

When other American cities saw how the people loved the Liberty Bell they asked to borrow it for their celebrations, too.

Its first trip out of Philadelphia was by train to New Orleans.

An Honor Guard went with it to the station. While a band played, it was carefully placed on a special flat car decorated with red, white and blue bunting.

After that, the bell traveled to many cities. Crowds and parades were always on hand to welcome it. Those who could not get to the cities lined the train routes to cheer and light its way with bonfires as it rolled past.

In 1915 the committee in charge of the famous bell decided it should not travel any more. Even with careful handling the crack might lengthen.

When San Francisco asked for the bell, the committee said, "No."

A storm of protest rose all over the country. Two hundred thousand children in California signed their names and asked the committee to please send the bell.

Finally the committee agreed and special preparations were made to insure its safety for its last trip outside the city.

It began its 10,000 mile journey with a mammoth parade through the streets of Philadelphia. For the first time, the bell rode in an automobile.

-2

When the Liberty Bell returned, it was placed lovingly in a spot of honor in Independence Hall.

Thousands of people from all over the world visit it every year.

Next to our flag it is our most treasured symbol of patriotism.

The company in England who first made the bell in 1752 has offered to recast it, but America has not accepted. The Liberty Bell in its present form tells the world of Freedom and Liberty more surely than if it spoke in round full tones.